T'CHALLA RULES!

A critical and cultural phenomenon, Marvel Studios' *Black Panther* has broken box office records and redefined the Super Hero movie for a new generation.

Black Panther: The Official Movie Companion offers an in-depth look at the creation of the acclaimed movie as told by the cast and crew who brought Wakanda to life.

CONTENTS

VIBRANIUM AND WAKANDA

A small, unassuming country in the heart of Africa, Wakanda has guarded a secret for thousands of years.

Millions of years ago, a meteorite made of vibranium – the strongest substance in the universe – crashed into the continent of Africa, a location now known as the country of Wakanda.

In Wakanda, five tribes were constantly at war with each other, until the Panther Goddess Bast decided to settle things by creating a Heart-Shaped Herb which would give a person superhuman abilities and become the Black Panther – Wakanda's protector and benevolent ruler…

The vibranium also allowed the country to significantly advance its technology and weaponry. The people of Wakanda chose to cut themselves off from the rest of the world, hidden behind an invisible barrier. From the outside, Wakanda is seen as a simple country, populated by farmers – but the real Wakanda is a futuristic city.

However, whether it's right to keep such technology and knowledge secret and exclusive to one hidden country is set to become a bigger question – and the cause of a whole lot of trouble for T'Challa and the people of Wakanda. ∎

A HERO RISES

It took his father's death for Prince T'Challa to inherit
the mantle of the Black Panther – the noble protector
of Wakanda. But for his first battle, he was not alone.

02

During a fierce battle between the Avengers and Hydra agent Brock Rumlow, otherwise known as Crossbones, in Lagos, Nigeria, several Wakandan humanitarian workers are accidentally killed. This leads to a proposal to impose United Nations sanctioned controls on the superteam – the terms of which are set to be negotiated at a conference in Vienna. King T'Chaka and Prince T'Challa of Wakanda are present at the conference, where T'Challa makes it clear, in a conversation with his father and Natasha Romanoff (the Black Widow), that he is not a fan of politics and diplomacy.

King T'Chaka gives an impassioned speech at the conference, backing the actions of the United Nations and offering Wakanda's full support. During the speech, T'Challa notices a commotion outside, before an explosion shatters the building.

T'Challa leaps to protect T'Chaka, but the King is killed by the blast. Seeking revenge, T'Challa vows to kill the man he believes responsible for T'Chaka's death – a brain-washed James 'Bucky' Barnes, now known as The Winter Soldier.

Unfortunately for Barnes, with T'Chaka's death T'Challa becomes the Black Panther, a man with enhanced speed, strength, agility and instincts, who wears a vibranium suit fitted with retractable claws.

The hunt moves to Bucharest, where Black Panther chases the Winter Soldier through the streets – with anything in their way becoming collateral damage. Captain America and Falcon attempt to halt the chaos, and the four men are eventually stopped and apprehended by War Machine, who is acting on behalf of the authorities. Black Panther removes his helmet, revealing himself to be Prince T'Challa.

With T'Chaka's death T'Challa becomes the Black Panther, a man with enhanced speed, strength, agility, and instincts.

03

04

T'Challa explains the nature of the Black Panther to Captain America and the Falcon – that the Panther is the protector of Wakanda, and a mantle which is handed through generations, from warrior to warrior.

Captain America – discovering that Barnes is innocent of the bombing – vows to protect his former friend.

The Avengers face their own internal civil war that pits Captain America, Falcon, Scarlet Witch, Hawkeye, and Ant-Man against Iron Man, Black Widow, War Machine, Vision, and Spider-Man. Black Panther chooses to join Iron Man's side. During the confrontation, Black Widow helps Captain America and Barnes to escape, but they are secretly followed by T'Challa. Later, as Captain America, the Winter Soldier, and Iron Man fight in a Siberian Hydra facility, T'Challa apprehends the real instigator of the troubles - and his father's death - Helmut Zemo. The Wakandan prince makes the noble decision to stop Zemo from killing himself and face justice.

Barnes is put into a cryogenic sleep until a cure can be found for his brainwashing – and T'Challa grants him asylum in Wakanda. ■

01 The Black Panther, a role passed down through the generations. (See previous spread)

02 T'Challa faces difficult choices as his reign begins.

03 The sworn protector of the people of Wakanda, the Black Panther.

04 T'Challa's high-tech vibranium-weave suit is bulletproof and fits into the teeth of his necklace.

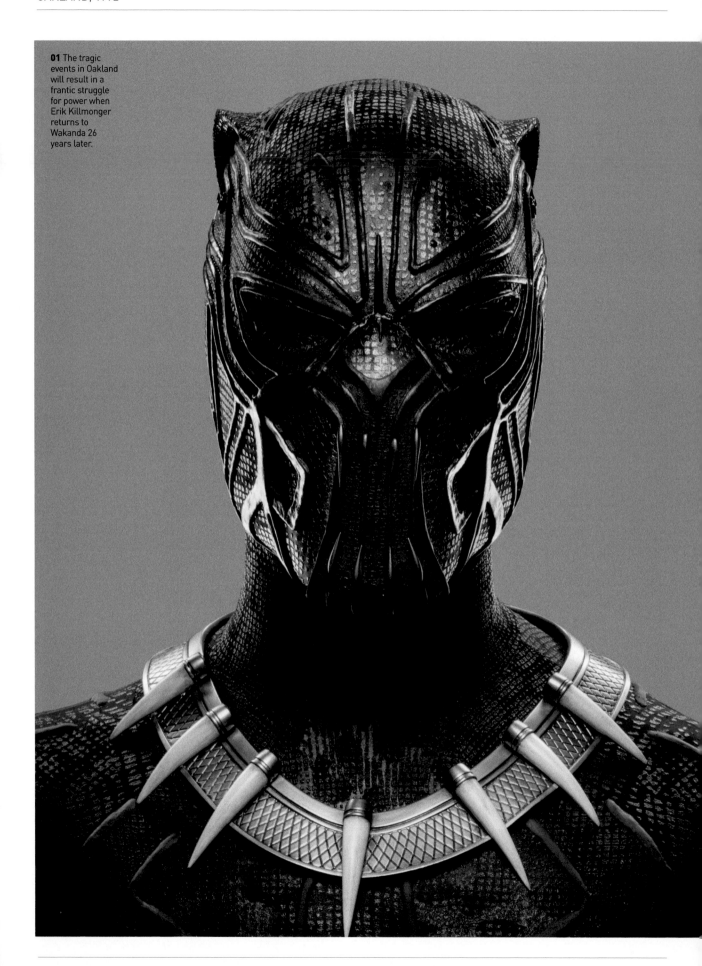

01 The tragic events in Oakland will result in a frantic struggle for power when Erik Killmonger returns to Wakanda 26 years later.

OAKLAND, 1992

The seeds of the tale are sown in a powerful prologue that takes place thousands of miles from the idyllic Wakanda, in a foreboding apartment block on the West Coast of America. Sterling K. Brown plays N'Jobu, whose political views contrast sharply — and tragically — with those of his brother.

Black Panther: The Official Movie Companion: What appealed to you about *Black Panther*?

Sterling K. Brown: It's a piece of movie history. It's a predominantly African/African-American cast in a Marvel Super Hero picture with Ryan Coogler as the director.

I have two kids, a five year old and a one year old. I took my eldest son to go see Marvel Studios' *Captain America: Civil War*. To see someone who looks like you occupying that role of being larger than life, like Chadwick Boseman does as Black Panther, is important. I'm pleased to have the chance to be a part of something that is incredibly empowering for a people that haven't had that opportunity yet.

What is N'Jobu's relationship with his brother like?

N'Jobu and T'Chaka are brothers but they have a fundamental difference of opinion on how they see the world. N'jobu is a war dog; he's essentially a spy that's been stationed in the United States for quite some time. He is somebody who is eager to be a catalyst for change.

T'Chaka is more nationalistic in terms of Wakanda first but N'Jobu''s views are much more globalized in terms of all people of African descent having a sense of responsibility. We can't just protect people within our borders without giving some sort of attention to those people who exist outside. I think it feeds from what's going on in our world now.

How was the experience of working with Ryan Coogler?
I love that dude. He's fantastic. He's one of the greats. He cares about every detail of filmmaking.

And he relates to everyone the same way. Crew, cast or whoever, there's no hierarchy with him. He looks you in the eye. He talks to you. He lets you know that he needs you, you need him, and everything is a collaboration.

Ryan has such a fond memory of being an Oakland kid in the early 1990s that he is just being immersed in that world. All I had to do was listen to Ryan really, and I just fell into that specific period automatically.

How did you achieve the effect of the vibranium tattoo inside your mouth?
I tattooed my lip... Just kidding, I did not tattoo my lip just for the movie! We used a little CGI magic. I pull my lip down, and the crew have a blue light that they shine on the inside of my mouth. And then the visual effects artists added the tattoo in post-production. ∎

WAKANDA

A HIDDEN KINGDOM

Creating a world the likes of which audiences have not seen before proved to be a rare challenge, even for Marvel Studios' *Black Panther*'s production team. Executive producer Nate Moore, line producer Jeffrey Chernov, production designer Hannah Beachler, and dialect assistant coach Atandwa Kani explain what they did— For Wakanda!

"Wakanda is pulled from Marvel Comics and the real world."—Nate Moore

Black Panther: The Official Movie Companion: How did you approach creating Wakanda?
Nate Moore (executive producer): Black Panther's a character that's been around since the 1960s, so there was a lot of great material to pull from. But Ryan Coogler had a lot of his own ideas of how to make this character couched in actual African culture. Something that was really important to us was to make Wakanda feel like a place that could exist on Earth rather than being a fantasy land. Part of that is achieved by building sets. Another part of that is looking for cultural references that are very real and very alive in Africa and building that into the story. So the world of Wakanda, and the idea of a kingdom with many tribes that make up the population of Wakanda are all things that were both pulled from Marvel Comics and the real world.

Then we used a variety of shooting techniques to put you into that, including drones, underwater shots, and 50-foot techno crane shots. But there's also a lot of handheld camerawork. It's something I think that Marvel Studios has developed over the years so that the stories can be epic but also really intense and personal.

Was previous experience useful on such a large undertaking?
Jeffrey Chernov (line producer): I felt that I could be valuable in the process of creating Wakanda, having worked on movies like *Tomorrowland* and the *Star Trek* movies. I felt like it was something I had done before, and something I enjoyed doing. So we sat and talked about it, and I

explained to them what I had learned in the process previously. It's a very complicated procedure that involves asking a lot of questions and then trying to figure out how you want to show a place that no one has ever seen before. Wakanda is technically advanced, but what does that mean? It can't be just a bunch of flying ships around a city. We needed to be able to get to the heart of it. We had to ask ourselves, who are the people of Wakanda? What do the people of Wakanda do? And how are they so technically advanced and different from the rest of the world?

We had to decide what was the most important part of the place – its heartbeat – and convey that to the audience.

We need to consider things like where do people live? What do they eat? What do they use for currency? All these things can be ▶

01 The instantly iconic
Wakanda, seen from the
air. (See previous spread)

02 Futuristic towers
dominate the
Wakandan skyline.

03 The man who would
be king: Killmonger
confronts T'Challa.

04 Nakia in Wakanda.

▶ important but they can sometimes be a distraction because it's not really where the story's taking you. So we needed to pick and choose what parts of the city to show and for what purposes.

Did you do a lot of research?
JC: I prefer not to. I prefer to leave that job to production designers, to costume designers, and to researchers. I just want to feel like the audience - and to leave the question of "would this really be possible or not possible" to the designers.

The fun is to have people show stuff to you and then let them look for your reaction.

05 An aerial view of the Wakandan capital.

06 A behind the scenes shot of Chadwick Boseman and Forest Whitaker.

What was your reaction to the sets?
JC: It's always tricky when you're creating a new world. You probably throw out a lot more than you keep in. It's just part of the process. In order to find the color palette or the architecture or the overall vibe of what a place should feel like, you need to put in a lot of work.

The point of departure is usually trying to create a skyline. It's a silhouette of what Wakanda is. A lot of time and effort gets spent on that, and it takes a while to get people comfortable. The skyline is whatever the heart of the city is. Look at Manhattan's

skyline or in *Star Trek* when we created a skyline in San Francisco. Or *Tomorrowland* when we created Tomorrowland. We always started with that silhouette from a distance. And then you gradually work your way in until you are actually standing on the street.

It's very hard because there was a nervousness about stepping onto the streets of Wakanda. We had to be careful that it works for the story. When we go into Wakanda there are areas that are different parts of the city that all tell a different story.

Some of the design was filtered out, and other parts got pushed

> ## "Wakanda is the the oldest city in the oldest country."
> —Jeffrey Chernov

to the side because they're not as important.

Why is the authenticity important?
JC: Wakanda is the birth of the world. It's the oldest city in the oldest country. It has had advanced technology for a long time.

What you might have thought came from somewhere else actually came from Wakanda. So music, language, dance, fighting styles, all filtered out into the world.

How did you research for
Black Panther?
Hannah Beachler (production designer): We visited South Africa and saw what architecture of the future looks like there. We tried some different ideas from what is canon to the comic and that gave us a little bit of a freedom. I wanted to push the envelope as much as possible.

How did your conversations start?
HB: Ryan was in Africa and was sending me pictures of the bells on people's ankles, pictures of shells, pictures of what people were wearing, and of different masks. He sent me videos of all kinds of technologies, such as future technologies and wearable technologies. And we talked about how to incorporate this into our world. Ryan is a very visual person, so I knew that's how we would work together, by seeing things and looking at different textures and colors.

"I wanted to have big things to destroy!" —Hannah Beachler

How did the color palette of costumes dictate your work?
HB: Ruth Carter [costume designer], Ryan and I had this impromptu long meeting, and we went through all her references and all my references. We talked very casually about what we liked, what we didn't like, the colors that we liked, how we wanted to create our own tribes and the traditions that we thought were important that we wanted to carry on in the film. It was very collaborative. Ruth would create her looks and she'd always want to know what colors I was using. I'd send her the palettes, and she'd sometimes come back asking for changes so that the colors worked on screen.

Did the large scope of this shoot dictate the size of your sets?
HB: It did to some extent because I was working in places that are just big anyway. They needed to be big and I wanted to do big. Every department played a large role in what these sets would be. The design was just crazy as

I watched it go from paper to reality – to actually being able to walk on the sets. I had a couple of moments where I had to tell everybody to leave the set for a second, to just let it all sink in, because this is the biggest thing I've ever done. It's been really crazy.

The stunts have also been important to me because I wanted to have beautiful things to destroy – that's what we love to see in the movies! So I've approached a lot of it as an audience member, thinking about what I would like to see in a Marvel film and making sure that we do it. We also have to account for lots of sweeping camera moves, and lots of beautiful scenery.

The language of Wakanda is Xhosa, a South African-derived dialect. How did you maintain a sense of authenticity?
Atandwa Kani (dialect assistant coach and cultural consultant): As a cultural consultant I was there to verify certain rituals, cultures, and things that would

07 Behind the scenes as the king takes to the throne.

08/09/10 Intricate sets help create a believable but fantastical world.

11 Daniel Kaluuya and Danai Gurira on set.

"I was teaching the actors songs, and call and responses." –Atandwa Kani

12 Away from the capital, M'Baku's icy domain shows a different side of Wakanda.

13 The stage hosting M'Baku's throne room.

14 The Jabari city, located within an icy mountain landscape.

15 T'Challa is taken to the Jabari to recuperate.

▶ and wouldn't be done by members of the Xhosa community. You need to accept that there's artistic license sometimes. The truth is we're shooting a film.

You also play a key role in front of the camera, don't you?
AK: I play King T'Chaka when he was a younger man at the start of the movie. My real life father, Dr. John Kani, plays the older T'Chaka. In fact, he introduced Xhosa as the language of Wakanda in *Civil War*.

Xhosa is an existing language in South Africa, spoken on the Eastern and Western cape.

Did you rehearse with the actors?
AK: We had scenes where there are large numbers of people. When I was not on set working with some of the actors on their accents, I was teaching the actors songs, call and responses, and chants.

I had to get that into their blood; it's not something that you can switch on and off. If I got a little

moment with a group of people, I'd teach them a song. They picked it up so quickly.

What do the chants signify?
AK: Strength, unity, and a bright future. The Xhosa people are from South Africa which has had a difficult past. What got us through those times was always dreaming of a brighter future. Wakanda doesn't have that same history, but these gestures signify moving forward and always calling back ancestors and realizing we are not alone. You can always rely on the next person. You'll never be left behind.

The purpose of these songs and these chants is that even if you don't understand the words, you feel what it's about. ∎

15

LONDON
A THREAT REVEALED

Few films offer as strong an introduction for their bad guys as Marvel Studios' *Black Panther*. Andy Serkis and Michael B. Jordan discuss their struggle against T'Challa.

01 Klaue (Andy Serkis) gets his claws on a Wakandan artefact. (See previous spread)

02 London's Museum of Great Britain faces an unusual robbery.

03 Only one of the priceless exhibits is the target of a daring heist.

Black Panther: The Official Movie Companion: What was your initial exposure to the world of Marvel? Andy Serkis (Ulysses Klaue): I saw *Iron Man* and I thought it was absolutely brilliant. It has such a great balance of humor, great storytelling, spectacle, and really interesting characters.

Did you look to the comic for inspiration in playing Klaue?

AS: I did. The basis of the character is all there, so I dove in as much as I could in the time that I had.

What did you enjoy most about working with Marvel Studio's *Black Panther*'s director, Ryan Coogler?
AS: He was such an extraordinary force on set. He's a really natural leader without having to be over-authoritative. He's all about character. He knows this world so well. It was really fun to work on this movie. He allows

actors to come up with their own ideas.

How do you keep things fresh with this character?
AS: Klaue is really enjoying his new weapon and his new life. He lives for the moment. I think there was a lot of humor in the way that Ryan and I worked on the character together.

Klaue wants to get as much money as he can. He's a total super capitalist. He wants the vibranium

03

> 05

"As a kid I always wanted to be Black Panther."
- Michael B. Jordan

▶ even if it means causing huge amounts of damage and death.

What is Klaue's relationship with Killmonger?
AS: The story is set up that everyone is focused on finding Ulysses Klaue. He is seen as a terrible danger. He's a real threat to Wakanda. He thinks he's using Killmonger and manipulating Killmonger, but it transpires, of course, that it's the other way around.

Did you do much stunt-training for the film?
AS: I did a little bit. I was mostly firing weapons, so I didn't have to receive too many of the hits – unlike my fellow castmembers! As Klaue makes his escape from the museum, there's a lot of gunfire as he gets rid of security guards and covers his tracks. It was a pretty physical role. Later in the story, when he's escaping from Killmonger, it got pretty physical. In fact, that was physically tiring and I actually got knocked about during that scene quite a bit.

How was Klaue's new weapon realized?
AS: In essence, it's a bionic arm. It has seams which unfold and click open. It goes from looking like a prosthetic arm and then it folds over and splits and the sonic disrupter comes out. It's an old mining tool from Wakanda, which Klaue had adapted.

What's it been like working with such an impressive cast?
AS: It was extraordinary to work with Lupita Nyong'o and Danai Gurira, and Chadwick Boseman and Martin Freeman. It was just a remarkable team.

Did you have a favorite Marvel character when you were growing up?

04 Klaue's raid on the museum called for much physical action.

05 Erik Killmonger assists as Klaue goes after the vibranium.

06

> "When you get everybody in the cast in one room, I'm always gauging for reactions." - Michael B. Jordan

Michael B. Jordan: Wolverine was a big character in my upbringing, Magneto as well. I always loved Magneto's sensibility of doing whatever's necessary to see change. But he also understood the humanity aspect of it as well. He kinda played both sides of the fence. He just had a different philosophy than Charles Xavier.

As a kid I always wanted to be Black Panther, even as recently as when Marvel Studios started up with the Avengers movies. I was always thinking, *I just need to get old enough to be able to play T'Challa.*

What did you like about Chadwick's take on Black Panther?
MBJ: I think it was just very honest. He did the work. I like the way Marvel rolled out the character. It all fits into their overall plan. So when you see certain characters pop in and out and the little breadcrumbs, especially if you're familiar with the comic books, you look forward to seeing them connect the dots.

Was it important that Killmonger's point of view was well-developed?
MBJ: Yes. It also makes it tough to know who you want to root for. You can see where everyone's coming from.

What was it like when you read through the script with the rest of the cast for the first time?
MBJ: The table read is fun. You get a chance to hear the words come to life. When you read in your head, your imagination runs wild and fills in how you think the dialogue should be said or how scenes are going to be played. But when you get everybody in the cast in one room I'm always gauging for reactions. I'm glad I first appear later on in the movie, as it meant I could hear how everybody was playing the scenes. It was like, *Okay, everybody's reading at 70%...*

You never know how hard you want to go in at a table read. You know, you got some guys that are up there like really going at it. And it's like, whoa, relax, buddy! We're not even on set yet. But then there's other times where, you know, everybody's just really laid back. So it's always interesting. ■

06 Regular workmates Jordan and Ryan Coogler on set.

07 Erik Killmonger eyes a piece of his heritage.

BUSAN
THE THRILL OF THE CHASE

Place your bets as stunt coordinator Jonathan Eusebio, special effects coordinator Jesse Noel, executive producer Nate Moore, supervising location manager Ilt Jones, and actors Danai Gurira and Martin Freeman take us through the action in Busan.

Black Panther: The Official Movie Companion: What were the technical aspects of the South Korean sequence of the film?
Jonathan Eusebio (stunt coordinator): The Busan sequence was one of the marquee action scenes for the movie. Our leading characters chase down Ulysses Klaue, meeting Everett Ross on the way. There's a brawl that takes us from the casino to a big car chase through the streets of Busan.

What kind of efffects were called for in this sequence?
Jesse Noel (special effects coordinator): We set up close to a thousand bullet hits to simulate gunfire from the bad guys. So we had breakaway bottles all along the bar, and we had debris falling and flying all over the place. We had poker chips flying from the tables and there were lots and lots of sparks. It's a very exciting sequence.

We had breakaway sets that the stunt performers tumbled through and breakaway railings up high so people could fall over the balcony.

What did the casino sequence entail?
Clayton J. Barber (fight coordinator): We had the four principal actors fighting. We were exposing them to a lot. It's a much more organic fight scene, prior to us seeing the powers of what these guys can really do. And then we had some bigger gags because Klaue played into this scene in a big way. You got to see him use his arm weapon for the first time.

The characters are wearing their normal clothes, so they seemed more human and vulnerable. But then there was also some Super Hero action. It made it a very eclectic and diverse scene in the sense of what you're able to do with the action.

What were the biggest challenges involved in creating such an action-packed scene?

"We just wanted controlled chaos on the set."
- Jonathan Eusebio

01 The Black Panther in hot pursuit! (See previous spread)

02 Marvel legend Stan Lee films his customary cameo appearance alongside Chadwick Boseman.

03 Boseman, Danai Gurira, and director Ryan Cooglar share a joke on set.

04 Andy Serkis prepares to unleash Ulysses Klaue on Busan.

JE: We rehearsed the sequence for about two weeks, setting up the camera shots because, ambitiously, we were trying to set the scene up as one continuous shot. It took a lot of prep time just to get a two to three-minute sequence looking like one long shot.

How many different shots combined into the one shot?
JE: We had about four to five stitches. Stitches are where we blend the individual shots together.

Did the actors do their own stunts?
JE: Yes. The actors trained really hard, so everything you see is all them.

One mistake can mess up the whole piece, so everything has to come out right. The performance has to be correct, the lighting has to be correct, the camera moves have to be correct, the special effects have to be correct. If one thing goes wrong then everything goes wrong.

For example, we had a camera move that followed a gunshot, up to the balcony, which started a stunt sequence for Danai Gurira as Okoye on the third level of the casino. As she fought, she leapt down to the second level, which involved another kind of camera rig. We tried to make it seamless as we're going up and down this whole casino.

This was the first time you see the cast fighting together and so it set the tone for action in the rest of the movie. ▶

04

"To Okoye, hair on the head is a disgrace!" - Danai Gurira

▶ **How many stunt performers did you have?**
JE: We had 15 henchmen, ten stunt patrons, six CIA. There were a lot of us in there. There's a lot mixed in with the background artists. The hard part was trying to organize it so the background performers didn't run into our stunt action. We didn't want to have to start the sequence all over again if something went wrong.

What was the hardest part of filming this sequence?
JE: A lot of it was just a matter of making it work for camera, keeping the energy up and then making it look like everything was as clean and frenetic as possible. It needs to be believable that this chaos is going on. We just wanted controlled chaos on the set.

Did any actors stand out as being strong stunt performers?
JE: Chadwick Boseman was really fast. He's been doing Martial Arts since he was a little kid. He's a really good Martial Artist. He's already a great actor, but he's also a great action star.

Lupita Nyong'o and Danai Gurira trained super hard. Any one of those guys can be an action hero. They're really good. They're all athletic. I think we're lucky that pretty much all our actors can physically do anything we ask them to.

What is Okoye's look?
Danai Gurira (Okoye): I had no hair for most of the movie, but it was really fun because there was a whole scene when I had to wear a wig.

It was a long, silky wig and Nakia says that it looks nice. Okoye thinks it's disgraceful, and I just love that. She has this really cool tattoo on her head and, to Okoye, hair on her head is a disgrace. I don't think we've seen that idea of turning the concept of femininity on its head before. It's very cool, because I do believe that she is deeply feminine. I totally see that she has an absolute sway in her hips and a confident, easy, feminine energy. She didn't forego that to be a woman of combat. ▶

05 Crowds gather in Busan to watch a Super Hero doing what he does best!

06 Nakai, T'Challa, and Okoye survey the casino.

07 Letita Wright behind the wheel as Shuri takes part in an unusual car chase.

05

06

08

Was it fun to bring back CIA operative Everett K. Ross?
Nate Moore (executive producer): There are fun character dynamics that we don't always get to play with. There's a really fun buddy dynamic between him and T'Challa. These guys that would seem to be adversarial, initially, find a common ground and are forced to work together to defeat the bad guys.

Is it a subversion of expectations that Ross is not a villain?
NM: I think government guys can be pigeonholed as suits who are there to obstruct. But what we found with Ross is that as much as

he felt like a suit in Marvel Studios' *Captain America: Civil War,* there's a real sense of nobility to him. I think that same sense of nobility is what draws him to T'Challa when the chips are down.

Is it a similar relationship to Phil Coulson and Tony Stark?
NM: A little bit, although Ross doesn't find himself the

butt of so many jokes in the way that Coulson did. I think there is a mutual respect there that allows these characters to play as equals rather than the mean way that Tony Stark sometimes treated Coulson.

How was South Korea as a location?
Ilt Jones (supervising location

"The locals were very jazzed [about Marvel Studios' *Black Panther*]." – Ilt Jones

> "Marvel Studios' *Black Panther* is the biggest movie to be shot in Busan by a large margin." - Ilt Jones

▶ **manager):** It was great. It was actually quite funny that we went from the crazy, nutty, anything-goes Africa to the sort of tightly wound – but very nice, I should add – South Korea. I think they've reached the 22nd Century ahead of the rest of us. Everything is 20 times faster than the U.S.! The broadband wifi speed is incredibly fast. South Korea is a highly technologically advanced country.

Were the locals receptive?
IJ: Absolutely. Marvel Studios' *Black Panther* is the biggest movie to be shot in Busan by a large margin. The locals were very jazzed about it. There were crowds on locations every night, cheering everything that was going on. There were ten straight nights of street closures.

Where does Everett K. Ross fit into all of this?
Martin Freeman (Everett K. Ross): It's enough dealing with a lunatic like Klaue, but Ross also has to deal with T'Challa, who is his ally in theory. But it's not like they're best buddies. He's still pretty much a loose cannon as far as Everett's concerned.

How was the casino shoot?
MF: I did weapons training, and I got quite good at it. I did about ten hours of work on it. I enjoyed doing it. As with everything in the film business, you have to prepare as much as you can. ■

12

12 T'Challa on the move as Chadwick Boseman dashes through the streets of Busan.

WARRIOR FALLS

A TALE OF TWO CHALLENGES

Two tense sequences featuring brutal fights against a backdrop of fast flowing water, hundreds of extras, and driving drum beats, are pivitol in Marvel Studios' *Black Panther*. Executive producer Nate Moore, actors Michael B. Jordan and Winston Duke, fight co-ordinator Clayton J. Barber, fight choreographer Jonathan Eusebio, and extra Rashida Abdullah share their perspectives as to how these show-stopping scenes were created.

Black Panther: The Official Movie Companion: Suprisingly, Warrior Falls was actually a set. How was it created?
Nate Moore (Executive Producer): Warrior Falls is an iconic Black Panther location from the comic book that we wanted to bring to life. We thought of a lot of different ways of achieving that. We looked at actually going to locations in Africa to shoot at a functioning waterfall. But the truth is that building it on a backlot allowed us much more control with visual effects, with stunts, and with special effects. So it made sense to build it in Atlanta, which has become our backyard.

Was it important that this was a functioning set as opposed to a blue screen set?
NM: It was fantastic to have a real, functioning set. It really helped us, and it helped the performers most of all. The cast really responded to the sets that were as three-dimensional as possible. It helped them to really inhabit the characters, and inhabit the world in a way that felt realistic for them and the audience. If we tried to do all this against a completely blue backdrop we wouldn't get the same kind of performance.

The set looked very dangerous, with gallons of water, actors fighting, and weapons being brandished. How did you ensure everyone was safe during the fight sequences?
NM: We did a ton of rehearsal in pre-production so that the actors knew all the steps to the fight. But it made a big difference once we were actually on a functioning waterfall set. So we had them rehearse on the set so they knew exactly where the footholds were and how to move in the water, and even how falling in the water felt. It was a very different

"I was feeling muscles I didn't know I had. My legs, my butt... everything ached!" –Winston Duke

experience working in those conditions than practicing all of that stuff in a stunt gym.

How was the stunt training?
Winston Duke (M'Baku): It was a lot of hard work! What's wonderful about this movie and really hard about it as well, is that we had a lot of moving parts. That's part of what's so brilliant about the Marvel movies. The fight scenes tell a story. My fighting style is different to T'Challa's. It's celebratory in a sense. The fight scenes are very involved.

I was going home and I was in pain. My back, my lower back was sore. My arms were sore. I was feeling muscles I didn't know I had! My legs, my butt... everything ached!

There was a lot of bow staff work. It started off quite flashy, and then devolved into what battle really is, which is dirty, messy, not too pretty, and dangerous.

What was it like shooting the fight at Warrior Falls?
WD: It was tough. I think I lost a pound per day working on that scene. It took a lot of energy putting out that energy, fighting in what is basically an arena, albeit a idio-syncratic arena, but still an arena.

Doing all that work over and over in the water that gives so much resistance was hard. The set builders were very specific and very realistic in how they designed the waterfall. It actually had uneven surfaces just like a real waterfall. Those elements contributed to the battle tactics in the scene.

How did you adapt as you filmed?
WD: We realized that we had to slow down because we could run in and hurt each other. I didn't want to slip. That went right into the battle tactics of having to fight and have the fight become something even more real. It completely evolved outside of the training room. It made the fight very authentic in many unplanned ways, and made it fun, real, and interesting. Every day was a new challenge and we welcomed it.

Did the drumming energy help you during the sequence?
WD: Yes. I don't think anyone was ready for the soundscape being another character in this movie. It informs what's happening. It's sharing things on. It's alerting you, warning you, harming you, and celebrating you. It has its own identity.

01 Ritual combat for the leadership of Wakanda. (See previous spread)

02 Killmonger strikes out as actors Chadwick Boseman and Michael B. Jordan showcase some amazing choreography.

03/04 T'Challa and M'Baku: rivals for the throne of Wakanda.

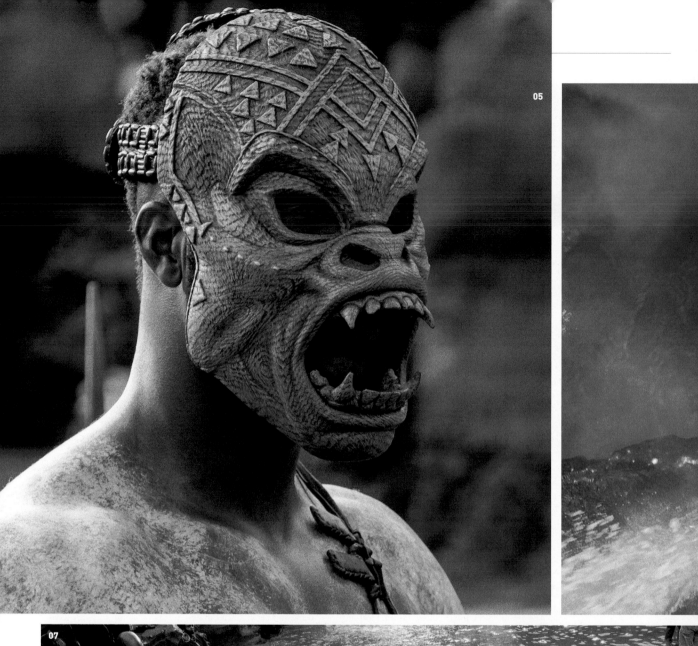

06

"The crowd adds a very important vibe to the scene." –Clayton J. Barber

It helped a lot in the scene, and it gave us energy. The Jibari drummers were completely different from the royal drummers, who are from Burundi.

How do you ensure the safety of the extras during this sequence?
Clayton J. Barber (Stunt Coordinator): We had a hundred extras up there, and we needed to pay attention to everyone. You're not allowed to make a mistake. You have to be conscious of that. We wanted to motivate them and encourage them to involve themselves in this scene because the extras are feeding the energy to the actors playing the parts that are living the experience. So the more you can involve the extras the better the two actors that are fighting can feed on the energy. The crowd adds a very important vibe to the scene.

How did you handle the water element?
CJB: We tested what we could do. But it was still a mystery of what could be done to make the sequence work. We thought that the water would be a beautiful thing. It would be a character in the movie because it would add flavor to the motion. It's beautiful to see water splashing up as the characters fight. We felt that, no matter what, we wanted to make sure that we were able to retain doing a fight in the water.

What was it like to participate in such an iconic fight?
Michael B. Jordan (Erik Killmonger): Warrior Falls was most definitely something I'd been looking forward to ever since I first read the script. Just trying to envision what it looked like and seeing graphic art for the sequence was nothing like actually seeing it up close and personal.

05 M'Baku at his most ferocious.

06 Victory for T'Challa as his foe yields... this time.

07 Ryan Coogler directs the Dora Milaje on the waterlogged set.

08

"Killmonger's been trained in everything." —Michael B. Jordan

▶ **How did you arrive at Killmonger's combat style?**
MBJ: I wanted to do something different than boxing. With *Creed* [Jordan's previous collaboration with Ryan Coogler] we made a statement and set the bar in terms of a fighting style. I wanted to do something different else. Killmonger's fighting style does not come from Wakanda. Everybody else is Wakandan for the most part in this movie. Killmonger doesn't know about tradition, only what he read. He's been trained in everything. He's picked up so many different styles along the way from fighting in America and Asia and Afghanistan and Russia. So that creates a clash of styles as Killmonger takes on T'Challa who uses the traditional Wakandan fighting style.

What's it like to be part of the Warrior Falls scene?
Rashida Abdullah (Mining tribe extra): I have been dancing since I could walk. My father is a world-renowned dancer, Baba Ali Abdullah. He was the chief choreographer for the National Ballet of Senegal for 16 years.

I found myself right next to the drums. I grew up with the drums. They are the heartbeat. It's a life force, it's energy giving. I don't think the movie would be the same without the drums, at least during that particular scene. The water is going and the drums are going... I was in heaven.

Was it a difficult set to work on?
RA: It had its challenges. I was quite high up, and when the water came rushing in I didn't realize that when we first started in the morning it would be cold. We had our coats that we'd put on and off again. It warmed up later. I appreciated that!

What were the differences between the two Warrior Falls sequences?
Jonathan Eusebio (Fight Choreographer): The first one is more about the pageantry, and it's the first time you're introduced to the world of Wakanda. You see this grand waterfall and you see the challenge. It's something that has been going on for thousands of years, their tradition. It's kind of primal combat, but you can see the beauty and the pageantry of the culture.   ▶

09

08 Erik Killmonger: "I've waited my entire life for this moment."

09 The waterfalls that offer a backdrop to violent confrontation.

10 T'Challa defends his right to rule.

"The first challenge feels like a sporting event, [the second] is more of a personal conflict..." —Jonathan Eusebio

11 Zuri officiates the combat at Warrior Falls.

12 Ryan Coogler offers Forest Whitaker some direction on set.

13 Rivals clash as T'Challa feels the wrath of his cousin.

14 Behind the scenes as T'Challa is bested as Zuri intervenes...

15 ...and the final shot with the background added.

▶ **Can you talk through M'Baku's challenge to T'Challa?**
JE: T'Challa's fight with M'Baku was choreographed with everything in grand, sweeping and even smooth movements. Even the way it was shot is different because there was a lot of crane movements or steadicam work where everything is steady and smooth to reflect the sense of water. The water gives a whole other visual element to the scene.

It's another obstacle that must be overcome.

How was Killmonger and T'Challa's fight different?
JE: The difference between that and the M'Baku fight is that the second fight is on a smaller scale in terms of spectators. But the emotion of that fight is very different. Whereas the first challenge feels like it's a sporting event, this one's more of a personal conflict

between the two. So the style of the shots is very different. Every-thing has a more handheld feel, it's more frenetic in its motions and rhythms.

What fighting styles did you use?
JE: There's a mix because certain African nations have different styles. Anywhere you go in the world there are different martial arts. You have to find the difference between martial arts and martial warfare. Fighting's fighting. If I put a stick in your hand or if I put a knife in your hand, you're going to start swinging it. So when it gets down to the bare characteristics of fighting, it's really primal. What makes each culture different is the pre-ceremony or the rituals before the fight. The mannerisms, stances, and the pre-rituals are all different. The ceremonies are all different. ■

14

15

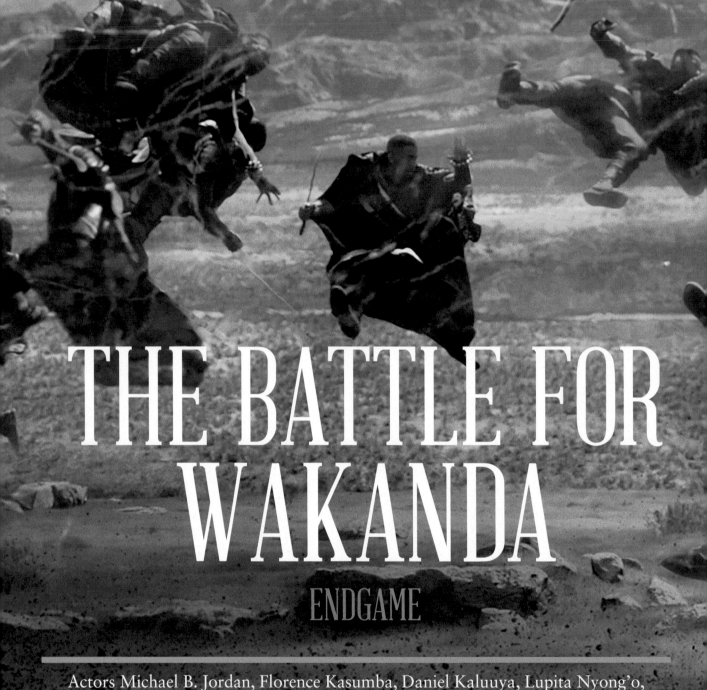

THE BATTLE FOR WAKANDA

ENDGAME

Actors Michael B. Jordan, Florence Kasumba, Daniel Kaluuya, Lupita Nyong'o,
executive producers Nate Moore and Jeffrey Chernov, supervising location manager
Ilt Jones, and production designer Hannah Beachler discuss Marvel Studios'

Black Panther: The Official Movie Companion: What is the relationship between Erik Killmonger and T'Challa like? Michael B. Jordan (Erik Killmonger): One was raised in comfort and one was raised on the streets and had to figure out things on his own. They both deal with loss. Erik's dad died and he had to go into foster care. T'Challa's father died and he became the king. He got a castle and a throne.

So I think there's jealousy and resentment there. T'Challa got the life that Erik could have had.

Did you enjoy the stunt training for the film?
Florence Kasumba (Ayo): That is

01 The Black Panther enters the battle. (See previous spread)

02 Killmonger is cornered by the Dora Milaje.

03 W'Kabi charges into battle astride a vibranium-armored rhino.

"Oh wow. I'm fighting the Black Panther... and not losing that much!"
– Daniel Kaluuya

the stuff that I loved the most about this movie because I train at home too. It was nice to not have to justify why I train so much anymore, because I was doing this movie. You have to look like the part. You have to be physically fit because we trained

for a long time and filming scenes took a long time. Sometimes you have to play a scene a hundred times, so you really need to be in good shape.

I loved filming the big battle at the climax of the film. It was a very long fight scene, but it was just amazing.

What was your approach to the fight scenes?
Daniel Kaluuya (W'Kabi): I was just learning what made it individual to the character and drawing from all kinds of fighting styles. W'Kabi is a warrior. He's quite ruthless and he can go toe to toe with anyone. But he doesn't show that he's a warrior. I tried to show that kind of confidence in him.

02

03

> "We had Atlanta doubling for the nation of Wakanda."
>
> - Nate Moore

▶ It's like when someone is really confident within themselves and within what they do. They're ready for anything. W'Kabi is adaptable like that. Whatever happens, W'Kabi's ready!

Do you have a favorite sequence?
DK: The W'Kabi Vs Black Panther fight was pretty cool. I can't lie. It was a pretty cool fight. It happened on my birthday so it was a pretty cool birthday present. I just thought to myself, *Oh, wow, I'm fighting the Black Panther... And I'm not losing that much!* I was actually going toe to toe with him. I managed to hurt Black Panther!

What's it like to be the top warrior of the river tribe?
Lupita Nyong'o (Nakia): I think that Nakia was born to be a warrior – she was born with a warrior spirit. Being the top warrior of her tribe is something that brings her a lot of pride. She's eager to make her people proud.

How did you realise the vibranium mound where the final confrontation takes place?
Nate Moore (executive producer): The vibranium mine is where all of the vibranium in the world comes from. So on this set we had a landing pad for different sorts of Wakandan aircraft, like the talon fighter and dragon fliers. We also had a lot of cases of vibranium.

This was actually a fantastic set built by our set designers in Atlanta, Georgia. So we had Atlanta doubling for the nation of Wakanda in Africa.

04 The Dora Milaje go before the camera.

05 The Black Panther unleashes some kinetic energy.

06 Killmonger dons ▶ a suit of his own.

"I wanted to make sure that there was vibranium everywhere."
- Hannah Beachler

What about the Wakandan countryside?
Ilt Jones (supervising location manager): We needed to try and emulate the savannah fields in South Africa, with those big open grasslands. We scouted the area just north of the Drakensberg Mountains and Johannesburg in South Africa. Ryan Coogler was immediately taken with that, so he wanted to use great rolling grasslands.

In Georgia there's a lot of forest. So that was a tricky one. But we found this place which had 8,000 acres of prime grassland. So it was a good fit for us. And the set builders created this amazing vibranium mine set on top of it. It made for a good synthesis between the natural terrain and the art department's ingenuity. And, of course, the visual effects team made it all join together seamlessly.

What helped tie the South Africa and Atlanta locations together?
Hannah Beachler: A lot of South Africa is red dirt, which luckily is prevalent in Atlanta as well.

How did vibranium play into your designs?
HB: I wanted to make sure that there was vibranium everywhere. It is a big deal in Wakanda. Captain America's shield is vibranium, and there was always that question, *What is vibranium?* It looks kind of like stainless steel to me. So I did some research into mining to try and discover what it would have to be.

07 Nakia joins the fight.

08 Chadwick Boseman films his scenes in Atlanta...

09 ... and the finished shot in the movie.

► I talked to a lot of experts in order to discover how this substance would originate, and how we would get it to this point. We added it into the sets in different stages. So you can see like what it is, what the color it is, what it looks like as a rock. Then once you start to mine it, what does it look like? And once we get through all the different stages of taking away the ore and all the metallurgy of it, then we can get it to a stainless steel look.

Why is it so important to shoot on location?
Jeffrey Chernov (executive producer): When you create someplace somewhere else, it's really important that everyone sees what it is you're trying to recreate. You can do it through

"I talked to a lot of experts in order to discover how [vibranium] would originate." - Hannah Beachler

photographs, and you can send scouts out there. But to really capture what it is you're trying to bring to audiences, it's really important to go there and see it for yourself. I worked on a movie a long time ago when I was an assistant director called *Escape from New York*. We never filmed in New York. I worked on a movie called *Battle: Los Angeles*. And outside of a day or two, we shot it in Louisiana. So I think that's

just the nature of our business, that when we are making these types of movies that have blue screen visual effects, to go to some of these places and to try and do what we do is just impractical. A lot of our films get made on back lots, or we go out to a ranch or a farm, something that has easy access, something that allows us to bring all the equipment that we need to be able to, again, tell the story. ■

10 Martin Freeman films his scenes from the safety of the studio.

11 City under siege - Wakanda comes under fire.

12 Action in the skies.

13 The final showdown!

13

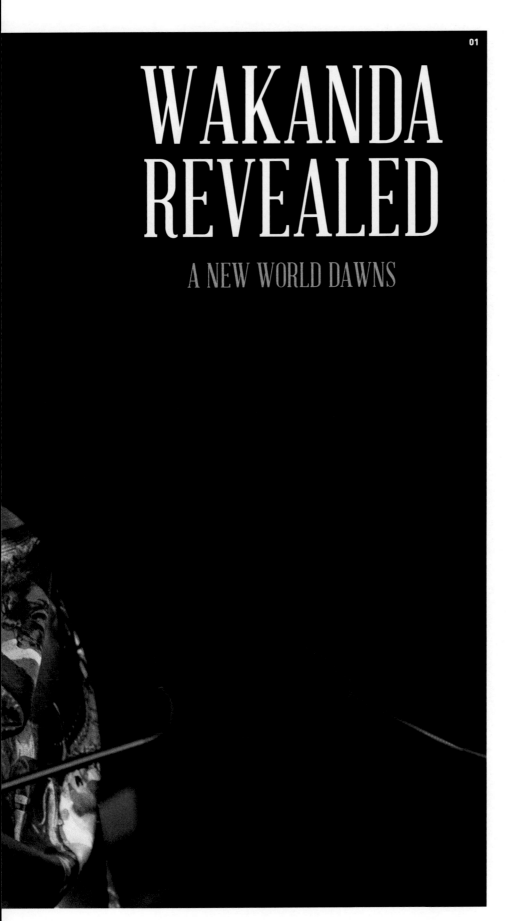

01

WAKANDA REVEALED

A NEW WORLD DAWNS

Actress Lupita Nyong'o discusses what makes Marvel Studios' *Black Panther* such a unique cinematic phenomenon.

Black Panther: *The Official Movie Companion:* **What makes Marvel Studios'** *Black Panther* **such a distinctive movie?**
Lupita Nyong'o (Nakia): Well, here we have a Marvel movie that is unapologetically black. And to see us occupy an African country with kings and queens and warriors – it's so inspiring. The cast that was put together to bring this Wakanda to life comes from all over the globe. We're talking Grenada, Trinidad and Tobago, Kenya, Uganda, Germany, America, England, South Africa, and Zimbabwe.

I think this film has made us look at the word diversity differently. I think diversity is often a word that we use to describe anything that's not white, but in this film we're talking about the diversity within an extremely large African population that has been brought together to bring this one nation to life. I think that's extremely important and something worth celebrating in and of itself. Africa is where the characters are from and that's how they identify. Getting the opportunity to film there, and seeing the people and the incredible locations was an amazing experience. ◼

01 T'Challa unveils the truth about Wakanda to the world.

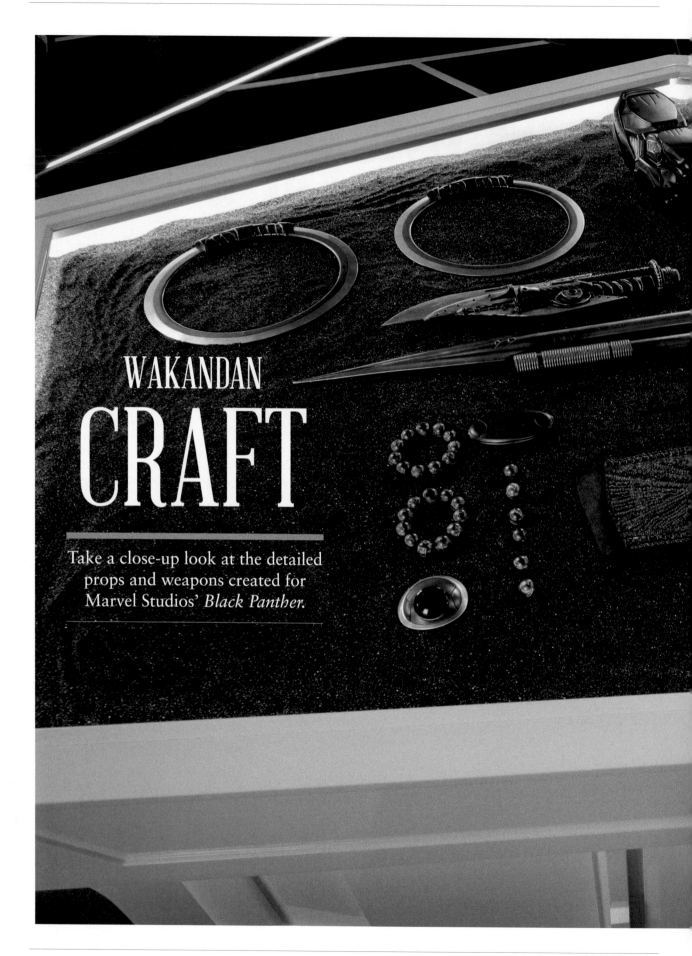

WAKANDAN CRAFT

Take a close-up look at the detailed props and weapons created for Marvel Studios' *Black Panther*.

01 An array of Dora Milaje weaponry as designed, in the movie, by Shuri. (See previous spread)

02 A detailed look at Shuri's ornate but powerful vibranium Gauntlets. They are panther-like gauntlets made of vibranium and able to fire powerful streams of energy.

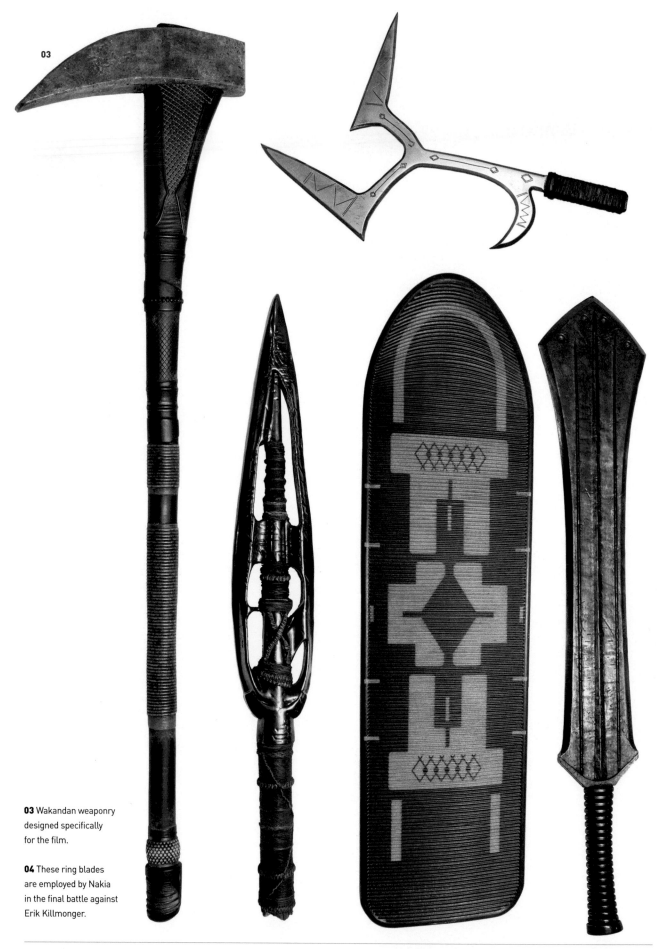

03 Wakandan weaponry designed specifically for the film.

04 These ring blades are employed by Nakia in the final battle against Erik Killmonger.

04

PRODUCTION ART

Marvel Studios' *Black Panther* called upon talented artists to realize the stunning vision of director Ryan Coogler and stay true to the iconic Marvel comic book.

04

05 Killmonger reigns! Art by John Staub

05

rodney.f

08

06 Killmonger: Armed and dangerous. Art by Rodney Fuentebella (See previous spread)

07 Killmonger: masked assasin. Art by Tully Summers (See previous spread)

08/09 The Black Panther suit in detail, and charged with kinetic energy! Art by Adi Granov

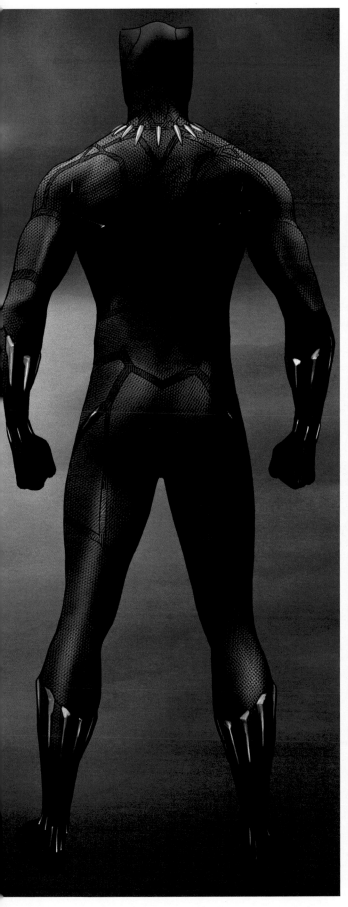

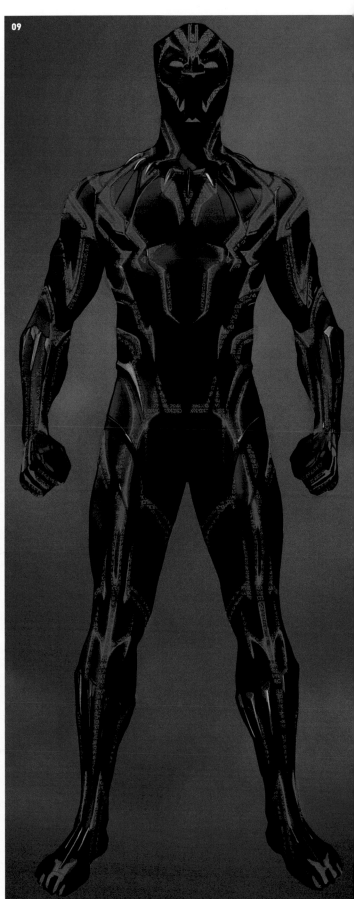

09

WAKANDAN STYLE

The Costume and Hair departments, headed by Ruth E. Carter and Camille Friend respectively, created amazing looks for the citizens of Wakanda.

Black Panther: The Official Movie Companion: Where did the working process on this movie start for you?

Ruth E. Carter (costume design): The script was changing all the time. I tried to keep very open and broad with the material and kept in touch with Ryan's aesthetic about what kind of cultural take on Wakanda he wanted to bring. It is Africa and it is based on tradition, we wanted to focus on that.

Were you afforded more freedom with your designs because Wakanda is a fictional world?

RC: Yes. However, we put a lot of thought into the costumes. I'm very particular about how people are dressed. So when they're a merchant, I needed to understand that they were a combination of two tribes from Africa. When they're from the river, I needed to know that they were in green and that they represented things from the water, such as fish and shells and things like that. I wanted the background characters to be as well dressed as the principals.

Did the stunts dictate the materials you used?

RC: That's the juxtaposition that we were dealing with all the time. The clothes sometimes had to be made to fight. We ended up making "tough suits" and "beauty suits." Sometimes they were created identically but the fabrics were a little heavier so that stunt performers could work in them.

What kind of color palettes did you use for the tribes?

RC: Ryan had a color palette that he designed. He really wanted to keep that color scheme very strict. When we see blue, it indicates that there is danger or trouble, so blue was kept separate for those tribes that either are a policing force like the border tribe or for Erik Killmonger's character.

The river tribe, which is Nakia's tribe, wears green. Nakia herself wears green, which includes a lot of camoflauge. Her tribe wears shells which reflect a closeness to nature. I also tried to bring in some things that support the greens, like yellows and chartreuse to make it more lush.

The merchant tribe wear a purple color, which is more of an aubergine kind of a purple. There is ▶

"I believe Danai's dress was by Stella McCartney... we took the sleeves off, and it looked incredible!" - Ruth E. Carter

01 Lupita Nyong'o as Nakia, wearing her tribal green. (See previous spread)

02 Okoye, dressed to kill in Busan.

03 T'Challa in his updated and improved Black Panther suit.

▶ also the mining tribe, which is what we call the combination of a farming tribe, which is Himba. They use the red brick clay, and so their color palette was orange.

What was Chadwick Boseman like to dress?
RC: Chadwick wears clothes really well. He's got square shoulders, is tall, and has a nice physique. He

works out all the time. He was very easy to dress.

Did you use anything from Marvel Studio's *Captain America: Civil War* into T'Challa's new costume?
RC: We used the *Civil War* suit in the very beginning of the film, and then we presented a new suit.

The Marvel illustrators did a beautiful job incorporating the

Wakandan language into the suit. T'Challa has a medallion on his chest that travels around his pectoral muscles and up around his upper chest. He wore a new necklace that feels very tribal as well. The latest suit was a little more streamlined, so we could do a whole lot more with less.

Okoye wears a spectacular dress in the Busan scenes.
RC: We had a great time working with Danai Gurira. I believe the dress she wore during that sequence was by Stella McCartney and it fit Danai like a glove.

She really wanted her arms to be exposed. So we had the sleeves taken off, and the dress looked absolutely incredible. ▶

> "Ryan had a color palette that he designed. He really wanted to keep that color scheme very strict."
>
> - Ruth E. Carter

▶ **What about Forest Whitaker (Zuri)?**
RC: We had very little time with each other. Sometimes the actors were fitted with a few days to go before they were on camera. Zuri's costumes were elaborate. Ryan was very influential in his shaman costume with the strips. Zuri's two costumes were created in Atlanta. We had a big shop cranking out stuff. Our specialty costumes were made in Los Angeles. Shuri's clothes at Warrior Falls and Great Bashinga were made from coast-to-coast.

What do you like about working with Marvel Studios?
Camille Friend (Hair department head): The creativity! Marvel Studios' *Guardians of the Galaxy 2* was a very creative experience. We established all these different universes. In Marvel Studios' *Black Panther*, we created Wakanda, putting together everybody's distinctive tribal looks.

What appealed to you about the project?
CF: It was really interesting that we would get to show what modern day Africa looks like because it is a mystery to so many people, especially if they've never been there. I've been to Africa twice, so I had a good sense of what people looked like.

The combination of making the actors look tribal and then fitting that in with what we could do within the Marvel Universe, was really exciting. ▶

What was your initial reaction to the film's script?
CF: I found it so interesting because it was totally about Africa. And they kept the very traditional aspects in. There was a lot of spirituality and a lot of mystical things in the film. On top of that, there was also the advanced technology that Wakanda has.

Ryan Coogler wanted to present a cross section of culture. I think this movie is definitely traditional. Then we had the modern, and then we have the advanced. That's how we took the approach with the hair. We combined all of those different looks throughout the movie.

Was it a challenge to include the different approaches?
CF: Actually, it really wasn't. As we got started, it was easy to figure out what would go where, depending on what was going to be in the script and how we wanted to go about it.

Did you look to the original comics for inspiration?
CF: Definitely. I initially looked

"Ryan wanted to present a cross section of culture."

– Camille Friend

---

at how all the characters looked in the comic books. Some of it we could use, some of it we couldn't, but we took as much inspiration as we could possibly get.

What were the conversations about the color palette?
CF: I like to start with thinking about what would look good on this person. If we part the hair to the left or the right – which is going to look better on their face? Sometimes we were sent sketches as suggestions from Marvel, but they were very open to letting us do whatever was really going to make everybody look their best on camera.

What were you especially proud of on the movie?
CF: We handmade all the tribal

stuff. I'm really proud of that. The different headpieces and different looks were created with different types of hair and product. We also used flowers and berries and curls and a wide variety of different fibers.

Were you afforded a lot of freedom as Wakanda is fictional?
CF: Yes. There were a lot of resource books and things that we shared generally. I looked at different tribes in Africa and found things that we could use that are real and worked it into our story. It was very rewarding to be able to do the research and learn so much about African culture and hair and the adornments.

Is hair design important to how we see a character?

04 Letitia Wright models a "funky" look as Shuri, coupled with her Panther gauntlets. (See previous spread)

05 Forest Whitaker as Zuri in his elaborate shaman outfit. (See previous spread)

06 Erik Killmonger shows off his gold detailed panther suit.

07 W'Kabi and his fellow members of the Border Tribe wear blankets that have vibranium woven into the fabric. This gives them shielding and cloaking abilites.

CF: That's what we tried to translate, especially when we were doing our bigger scenes toward the end on the barge. It's a celebration. So we really went all out to create elaborate hairstyles, to create elaborate hairpieces. And that's where we really got to showcase the hair in the movie.

The film features some intricately created wigs. What was the thought process behind these?
CF: We have the mining tribe, and they used red clay on their hair. All the hairdos that we used for them used a red clay. It took us weeks of research and development to establish a red clay that was really going to work on a wig or on someone's hair and not stain it.

For the river tribe, we used a lot of grasses, flowers, and natural tactile things like seashells to create different hairpieces and other small details. The border tribe favored haircuts that were more clean and militaristic. But on the women, we wanted to have a kind of modern up-do. We went for something more contemporary for those ladies.

How did you arrive at Nakia (Lupita Nyong'o's) look?
CF: We wanted to do something that was going to look really beautiful on her but also look natural. Ryan had said from the beginning that he wanted her hair to have color. So we went through several color tests and color matches until we came up with the color that she's wearing in the final film. But we wanted her hair to be natural, and that's how we came up with the little twist. Then in the casino scenes we made it bigger into a beautiful kind of asymmetrical Afro shape.

Angela Bassett (Ramonda) has a very distinctive look in the film. What inspired her style?
CF: From the very beginning of the process, I was thinking that we could create a silver dread wig. I thought it would look so dope

"I was thinking we could create a silver dread wig for Angela Bassett. I thought it would look so dope on her!"
— Camille Friend

on her! And Angela was all for it. That was probably one of our most expensive wigs, actually, because the dread locks were all handmade. I think there were 120 pieces that went into that wig. It was labor intensive to create, but the end result is really beautiful.

How did you arrive at Shuri's cooler hairstyle?
CF: Ryan wanted her to look funky, but still look African. We weren't sure what we were going do for her, initially. Finally, we settled on the braids and then we shaved the back and put a design in it to keep her looking really modern, young, and fresh.

Was it a challenge to create the Dora Milaje's style?
CF: It was a hard day when we shaved their heads. We took it very seriously. We were very patient with the actresses because it's a big deal to shave your head and know it will be shaved for

months. We got through all of that. All of the ladies playing the Dora Milaje were wonderful.

Were there any male looks that stand out as highlights?
CF: One of the coolest looks we did is Killmonger's look for Michael B. Jordan.

We had him grow his hair as long as he could, and then we added dreadlock extensions. That gave the character that totally different look so he really stood out as the villain.

Are there any hairstyles that you are particularly proud of?
CF: One of the looks that I really loved is Winston Duke's hair as M'Baku. We shaved his head and lightened his hair a little to give him a really strong Jibari warrior look. We talked about what we were going to do with his hair, and what was going to look good with his facial shape and his wardrobe. ■

08 Angela Bassett and Letitia Wright wear their carefully created hairstyles.

09 Danai Gurira shows off her Dora Milaje tattoo!

PRODUCING AN EPIC

CREATING A SUPER HERO MASTERPIECE

Producers Nate Moore and Jeffrey Chernov talk about the challenges and the triumphs in bringing Marvel Studios' *Black Panther* to the big screen.

01

What was the most exciting thing about making this film?
NM: I would have been into this movie if I were an audience member, more than anything else I've seen before. I was excited to be bringing a story like this to fruition and characters like this to fruition. I liked the idea of telling the story of an African king who's also strong enough, fast enough, and smart enough to be a Super Hero, but at the same time deal with some of the human issues that I recognize as a regular guy. What I was most looking forward to was sharing it with an audience and seeing how it impacted on the little kids who are like I was.

This was your first Marvel Studios movie. How did you find the experience?
Jeffrey Chernov (line producer): The Marvel Studios films are very successful, and they have a system that they like to work to, so it was different. Not having worked under that system meant an adjustment for me. With the type of work that I do I'm kind of the architect of the movie, even though Marvel Studios are the true architects. I'm an associate architect on this production.

What are the responsibilites of a line producer?
JC: Part of my responsibility is figuring out how to mount the movie. A lot of things were decided before I started on the film, like where we were going to shoot, and what time of the year we were going to shoot. In certain ways it was quite easy. I didn't have to deal with multiple schedules or multiple budgets.

How important is the storytelling?
JC: I think the most important thing is storytelling. Ultimately it's about the story, and it's about telling the best story. When you're making these big Super Hero movies you want to try and be true to a couple of things. One is that there has to be a certain amount of reality to it, because I don't think the audience want to see something that's too far out that they can't relate to. They ▶

Black Panther: The Official Movie Companion: The Busan casino scene has a James Bond vibe – was this intentional?
Nate Moore (executive producer): The Busan casino sequence was our ode to James Bond. A lot of James Bond sequences take place in casinos where you get to see him in his great suit. This was our version of that. King T'Challa leaves Wakanda for one of the few times in the film, and you see him interact with the outside world.

You had an editor on set. What was the significance of that?
NM: One of the challenges of an action sequence is making sure everything feels seamless, and one of the ways we do that is by having an editor on set, cutting footage in real time. This isn't something we do often at Marvel. But it's something that Ryan Coogler, our director, felt was the best way to ensure we captured all the action, all the stunts, and all the special effects in frame on time.

01 Nate Moore,
Chadwick Boseman,
and Ryan Coogler
work on a scene.

02

03

04

02 Ryan Coogler and Nate Moore on set.

03 Getting ready for action.

04 Michael B. Jordan and Chadwick Boseman film a tense confrontation.

05/06 Coogler works on scenes with Lupita Nyong'o and Letitia Wright.

▶ are willing to accept super powers as long as they make sense.

As a filmgoer, I always find that I get taken out of a movie or I get distracted by things that don't feel like they're real. So as a filmmaker that's what I would always try to prevent, and to make sure that the story is there. The action should be driven by emotion. If the characters are taking you on a journey then you should be able to feel their jeopardy and their victories. Action just for the sake of it doesn't work.

Was Marvel Studios' *Captain America: Civil War* a strong start for the Black Panther?
JC: It was great that Black Panther was introduced in a movie that gave him such a standout role. Losing his father really helped create a story for this one. It's a very important

part of this movie that is wrapped around an event that took place in the last one.

I think that when you start a franchise it's important to let that character stand on his own and then build the future around that.

How do you feel about the strong sense of diversity in the movie?
JC: The diversity of this movie is pretty amazing. We not only had a large Afro-American cast but our cinematographer, our director of photography, our production manager, and our first assistant director were all women. So I'm surrounded by a very diverse cast but also a number of strong-willed women in very important positions, and I'm really proud of that. I've not been on a movie that had so many women in key positions before.

Was the size of this project daunting?

JC: It's been an incredible experience to be able to put together something like this on such a large scale and on such a large budget. I take my hat off to Marvel Studios and to Disney for embarking on a project of this size, because it has never been done before. We actually created history. We created the first black Super Hero movie with a very diverse cast. We want to make more.

Did you have any problems shooting globally?
JC: I went on the location recce to South Africa, but I couldn't get in because my passport was so full. I knew that you need six months on the back of your passport to go anywhere. But what I didn't know was that you need two blank pages to get into South Africa. So I traveled 25 hours with a dozen people for this big scouting trip. And then when I got there, they turned me away.

So I had to head back to Los Angeles. I was waiting in the lounge for my plane, so I typed in U.S. Citizen travels to South Africa. And the first thing it says is you need six months on your passport. And the second thing it says you need are two blank pages. So, I spent 50 hours in three days traveling for no reason.

I went back to Los Angeles. A week later I could have flown over to meet up with the crew in South Korea. I just wasn't ready to get back onto an airplane at that point. I do not recommend flying 50 hours continuously. It's really horrible!

What was it like working with Ryan Coogler?
JC: If you add up his first two movies in terms of their cost and the length of time shooting, and then you talk about his third film, *Black Panther*, it's a quantum leap into

> "On these types of movies we're not sprinting. These are marathons."
> - Jeffrey Chernov

another type of filmmaking. That was one of the things that I was looking forward to, because I've had the experience of making these types of movies. When I met with Ryan I said that I'd like him to accept me as his pace car. On these types of movies we're not sprinting. These are marathons. Unlike his previous films, this was a design movie, meaning that everything had to be conceptually illustrated. Then we needed to translate that into actual practical costumes, props and sets.

I said to Ryan that he'd probably find that the decisions that

he would usually make maybe two or three weeks prior would have to be made two or three months earlier because the costumes would not be ready, the sets won't be completed and the props wouldn't have been made. You just have to get used to that. I guided him through that so that it wouldn't be an avalanche. With a project like this, you have to be prepared to have more questions asked of you in a day than you've probably ever had before.

That only intensifes as we got closer to shooting. It's like a boxer who is used to fighting ten rounds ▸

07 Directing
Danai Gurira.

08 Filming with
Chadwick Boseman
and Lupita Nyong'o. The
blue screen background
will be added later.

09 Chadwick Boseman
in front of the camera.

> "There's a heart
> and soul in Marvel
> Studios' *Black
> Panther* that came
> from having Ryan
> as a director."
> - Jeffrey Chernov

▶ and having to go 15. It's just a
different training program. I really
wanted to help him by preparing
him for all of the extra decision-
making that he would have to do on
the movie.

**What do you feel Ryan brought to
this film?**
JC: I think there's a heart and soul
in Marvel Studios' *Black Panther*
that came from having Ryan
as the director. I'm not taking
anything away from other Marvel
filmmakers, but I think what
brought Ryan to this project was
the previous films that he did. If
you watch them, you can see that
there's a tremendous amount of
heart and soul and attention to the
performances. I think that Ryan
will always look for that. No matter
what type of movie he's making,
he'll always demand that from his
own writing. He'll demand it from
his actors and from himself.

Sometimes action movies skip
over some of the more emotional
stuff, but not Marvel Studios' *Black
Panther*. It's Ryan's strength to tell
the story in that way. ∎

09

BLACK PANTHER

AROUND THE WORLD

As Marvel Studios' *Black Panther* ends, T'Challa reveals himself — and
Wakanda — to the rest of the world. But in real life, T'Challa's exploits are
very familar across the globe, having been translated into numerous languages.

Hungary

Poland

Taiwan

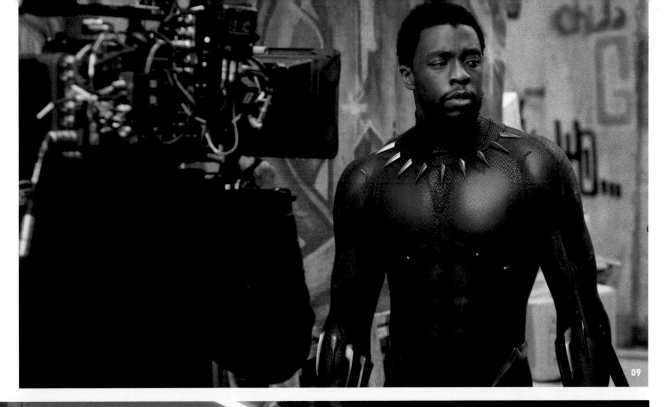

09

BLACK PANTHER

AROUND THE WORLD

As Marvel Studios' *Black Panther* ends, T'Challa reveals himself — and Wakanda — to the rest of the world. But in real life, T'Challa's exploits are very familar across the globe, having been translated into numerous languages.

Hungary

Poland

Taiwan

MARVEL
PANTERA NEGRA

Spain

MARVEL
ЧЕРНАТА ПАНТЕРА

Russia

MARVEL
PANTHÈRE NOIRE

France

MARVEL
ЧОРНА ПАНТЕРА

Ukraine

MARVEL
הפנתר השחור

Hebrew

MARVEL
ブラックパンサー

Japan

MARVEL
블랙팬서

South Korea

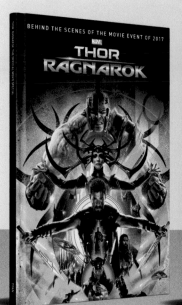

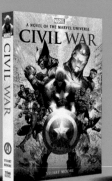

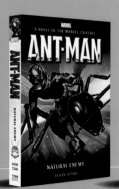